This Is My Truck

3 1389 01955 4567

By Amanda Hudson

Reading Consultant: Susan Nations, M.Ed.,
author/literacy coach/consultant in literacy development

WEEKLY READER®
PUBLISHING

Please visit our web site at www.garethstevens.com
For a free catalog describing our list of high-quality books,
call 1-800-542-2595 (USA) or 1-800-387-3178 (Canada).
Our fax: 1-877-542-2596

Library of Congress Cataloging-in-Publication Data

Hudson, Amanda.
      This is my truck/by Amanda Hudson.
          p. cm. — (Our Toys)
      ISBN-10: 0-8368-9255-0   ISBN-13: 978-0-8368-9255-0 (lib. binding)
      ISBN-10: 0-8368-9354-9   ISBN-13: 978-0-8368-9354-0 (softcover)
      1. Vocabulary—Juvenile literature. 2. Trucks—Juvenile literature. I. Title.
PE1449.H77   2009
428.1—dc22   2008002031

This edition first published in 2009 by
Weekly Reader® Books
An Imprint of Gareth Stevens Publishing
1 Reader's Digest Road
Pleasantville, NY 10570-7000 USA

Copyright © 2009 by Gareth Stevens, Inc.

Senior Managing Editor: Lisa M. Herrington
Creative Director: Lisa Donovan
Electronic Production Manager: Paul Bodley, Jr.
Designer: Alexandria Davis
Cover Designer: Amelia Favazza, *Studio Montage*
Photographer: Richard Hutchings

Printed in the United States of America

1 2 3 4 5 6 7 8 9 10 09 08

A Note to Educators and Parents

Learning to read is one of the most exciting and challenging things young children do. Among other skills, they are beginning to match the spoken word to print and learn directionality and print conventions.

The books in the *Our Toys* series are designed to support young readers in the earliest stages of literacy. Children will love looking at the full-color photographs while also being challenged to think about words that name objects and how those words fit into a basic sentence structure.

In addition to serving as wonderful picture books in schools, libraries, and homes, this series is specifically intended to be read within instructional small groups. The small group setting enables the teacher or other adult to provide scaffolding that will boost the reader's efforts. Children and adults alike will find these books supportive, engaging, and fun!

—Susan Nations, M.Ed.,
author, literacy coach, and consultant in literacy development

fire truck

This is my fire truck.

mail truck

This is my mail truck.

garbage truck

This is my garbage truck.

tow truck

This is my tow truck.

tanker truck

This is my tanker truck.

dump truck

This is my dump truck.

This is not a truck!